The hare-kin

HARE

written by Zoë Greaves

Illustrated by Leslie Sadleir

Old Barn Books

He is coming! O'Hare is coming this way!

Call him Hare King.

The hare-kin

 O'Hare's a hare; a golden hare, as rare a hare as any hare could be.

The swift-as-wind
The frisky one

Quiet now. You must not make a sound. Quieter still.

Can you hear a hare's breath?

Hide here in the scrub.

The low creeper

Look now. Look carefully.

Look still more harefully.

The stag of the cabbages

Long-eared

O where, O where is O'Hare?

Don't confuse him with a rabbit.

Hare was born with his clothes on, eyes wide and ready to go.

Nobody knows where he goes!
Hare today, gone tomorrow!

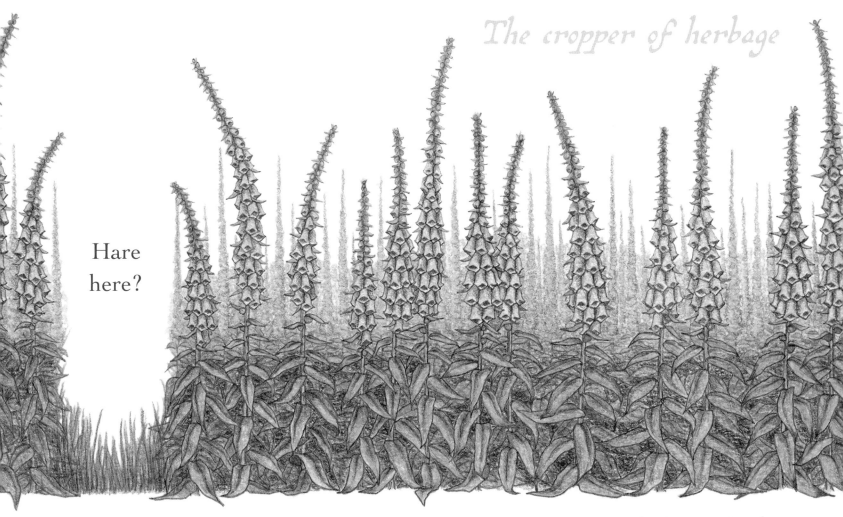

The cropper of herbage

Hare
here?

The hopper in the grass

Hare there?
HERE HARE!

The light-foot

O'Hare is here! Leaping there! Magnificent hare!

O'Hare hears. The get-up quickly

The fidgety-footed one

He was hare…

and now he's gone.

The fellow in the dew
The slink-away

Heir to the moon.

What is a Hare?

Hares are wild creatures that look a bit like bunny rabbits. They have long ears and very long back legs.

If you are very lucky, you might see some running across meadows or farmland.

Hares usually live alone although gather in large groups in the spring when the females can be seen 'boxing' the males with their front feet.

Most hares are nocturnal, meaning they come out at night.

There are about 32 different species of hare. They can be found all around the world except Antarctica.

The most common is the brown hare or European hare – but if you're an explorer you might also see a snowshoe hare (from North America), a golden hare (from Northern Ireland), a broom hare (from Spain), a Hainan hare (from China), an Arctic hare, or a mountain hare.

Confusingly the jackrabbit from North America is not a rabbit, but a hare!

Learn more about the hilarious hare by completing the fun activities on the following pages!

But first, can you draw a tail on this hare?

The Moon Hares

On a clear night you might be able to spot the shape of a hare on the moon.

The moon and the hare appear together in ancient stories from India, China, Africa, North America and Europe.

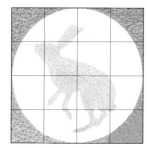

Using the small moon as a guide, can you draw your own hare in the larger moon? You could then colour it in.

The Easter Hare

For thousands of years, people have been telling tales about the hare…

It is said that the Anglo-Saxon goddess of spring, Ostara, once turned a bird into a hare – which then laid brightly coloured eggs. This is why, in Europe, the Easter bunny lays eggs. It's not a bunny – it's a hare!

Can you find all six Easter eggs in the picture and colour it in?

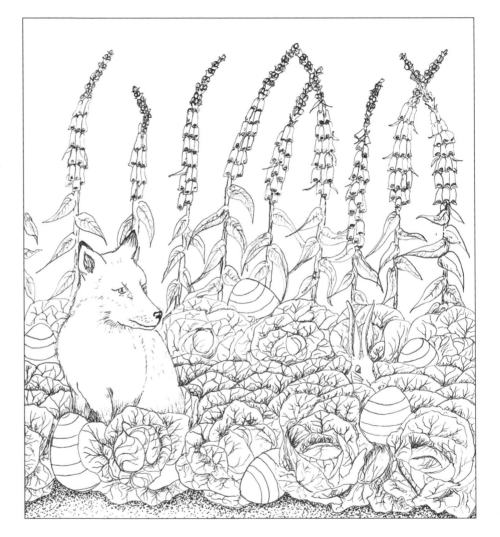

Tall Tales

Do you know the famous story of The Tortoise and the Hare? The hare is so sure that he'll beat the tortoise in a race, that he stops and takes a nap. Meaning the slow-and-steady tortoise wins instead!

Can you think of any more stories with hares? Which adventure does the mad March Hare come from?

Make up a story by filling in the gaps with your own words. There are no right or wrong answers. Just have fun!

Once upon a time a long-eared _____ was being chased by a ferocious _____. To escape, it hid among the _____ and soon became quite lost. The sky darkened and the _____ rose in the sky. The sounds of a _____ could be heard in the distance and our long-eared hero was quite scared. In the morning, a friendly _____ showed the way to safety with the help of a _____. With a hop, and a skip and a giant leap over the _____, everything ended well.

Trickster Hares

You may have heard of the character Bre'r Rabbit. He is a jackrabbit (an American hare) and is a true hero of folklore. Although smaller than his enemies (Bre'r Bear, Bre'r Wolf and Bre'r Fox), he manages to outwit them all!

Our own hare has also tried to outsmart you by hiding 10 words in this wordsearch. Can you find them?

OLDBIGBUM
FIDGETY
SWIFT
FRISKY
FAST

TRAVELLER
LURKER
CREEPER
HOPPER
SLINKAWAY

```
K V K U D R F S F R O Y
T Y I T K I S E E L A R
S B F J D N P L D W E E
A J S G V P L B A T U P
F U E S M E I K X F R E
J T T K V G N R M I K E
Y T G A B I Y E F W E R
H W R U L K S P Q S R C
A T M S S Z P Y Q V H
V T B I W P N O B Q I J
R F R M R T P H W W E F
O F O Z K I H A Y D X G
```

Lucky or Unlucky?

Throughout history, there have been many myths about the hare. Some people thought it brought good luck, while others thought it was not so lucky.

Can you follow the wiggly lines to find out which one is the lucky Chinese hare?

Sailors would return home if a hare crossed their path when they were setting out for their boats.

In China, it was once believed that the hare protected all wild animals. So it was thought to bring good luck!

A girl would delay her wedding if a hare hopped in front of her during her engagement.

It was thought to be unlucky for a pregnant woman to see a hare.

Many people once believed that witches could turn themselves into hares – so hares were often thought to bring bad luck.

The Stag of the Cabbages

Hares can reach speeds up to 45 miles per hour and can leap an amazing 2 metres high in the air!

Our own hare has managed to escape through this maze of cabbages. Can you find out which way it has gone? You'll have to be quick!

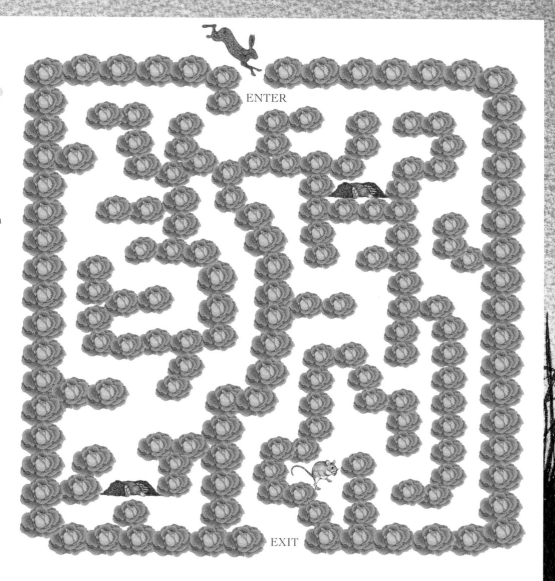

ENTER

EXIT

More Fun Facts!

Hares drum on the ground with their back feet
to warn others of danger.

Hares can use their powerful legs and feet to kick an enemy.

Hares usually feed on plants – grass is their favourite food.

Mummy hares can give birth to over 40 babies
in their lifetime! The babies can hop about
when just a few minutes old.

A hare under a year old is called a 'leveret'.

A group of hares is called a 'drove'.

Hares are usually quiet but will scream when frightened.

A hare's eyes are on the side of its head – so it can spot
danger from all around. Its large swivelling ears
also pick up warning sounds.

Hare or Rabbit?

Hares may look like bunny rabbits, but they are
different in many ways. Can you guess whether
each of these facts is about a rabbit or a hare?
(answers below).

1. They run fast over long distances

2. They dig underground dens

3. They have long legs

4. They like to eat in the middle of large fields

5. They prefer to eat close to home, in woods
or close to the hedgerow

6. They scrape shallow dips in the grass
where they hide from enemies

Answers: 1. Hare 2. Rabbit 3. Hare 4. Hare 5. Rabbit 6. Hare

Acknowledgements

"Hare" was originally inspired by the poetry of William Cowper (1731-1800)
and a fortuitous encounter with a huge, handsome hare on the outskirts of a wood in Worcester.
Which was more like being visited by a king. I later read a translation, from Middle English, of "The Names of The Hare".
These names, a mix of descriptive, respectful and insulting were recited by superstitious poachers for success and protection.
Zoe Greaves

This book is for V&B from Z&L

Moral Rights:
Leslie Sadleir has asserted her right under the Copyright, Designs and Patents Act 1988
to be identified as Illustrator of this Work

AN OLD BARN BOOK
First published 2014 by Ictis Books
First published in hardback in 2015 by Old Barn Books Ltd
This paperback edition published 2017 by Old Barn Books Ltd
www.oldbarnbooks.com
Illustration © 2015 Leslie Sadleir
Illustration page 18, Egg hunt © 2016 Lydia Ellwand
Text © 2015 Zoe Greaves

ISBNL 978-1-91064-611-3

10 9 8 7 6 5 4 3 2 1

Printed in Italy by L.E.G.O. Sp.A.

FSC
www.fsc.org

MIX
Paper from
responsible sources
FSC® C023419

Paper in this book is certified against the
Forest Stewardship Council® standards.
FSC® promotes environmentally responsible,
socially beneficial and economically viable
management of the world's forests.